FREAK

Riverhead Books
a member of
Penguin Putnam Inc.
New York
1997

John Leguizamo with David Bar Katz

A

Semi-

Demi-

Quasi-Pseudo

Autobiography

RIVERHEAD BOOKS
a member of
Penguin Putnam Inc.
200 Madison Avenue
New York, NY 10016

Library of Congress Cataloging-in-Publication Data

Leguizamo, John.
Freak : a semi-demi-quasi-pseudo autobiography / John Leguizamo with David Bar Katz.
p. cm.
ISBN 1-57322-092-2
1. Leguizamo, John—Biography.   2. Dramatists,
American—20th century—Biography.   3. Comedi-
ans—United States—Biography.   4. Hispanic Amer-
icans—Biography.   I. Katz, David Bar.   II. Title.
PS3562.E424Z47   1997   97-26289 CIP
812'.54—dc21
[B]

Printed in the United States of America
1   3   5   7   9   10   8   6   4   2

This book is printed on acid-free paper. ∞

Interior photos copyright © 1997 by Blake Little

Book design by Judith Stagnitto Abbate

ACKNOWLEDGMENTS

A very special thanx to Dave Bar Katz whose immense contribution and vision really helped this show come to life, especially when I was ready to quit; Justine Maurer, my cutie pie, who sacrificed many hours to my mistress, my art, and who encouraged me onward; much gratitude to my mother, Luz, and my brother Sergio for their patience and understanding and above all their forgiveness for letting me expose dirty laundry, 'cause God knows I wouldn't have allowed this to happen if the roles were reversed; to Aury Wallington for all her hard work, making all the details happen so the sum could be whole; to Dennis Brooks for all his help, Mike Carroll for more help; to Julie Merberg whose idea

Leguizamo

was this very book and whose hard work made it happen. To Gena Merberg who took some great shots for us; to Johnny and Hilary Reinis who believed in us and produced a very successful run in San Francisco; Mark Russell at PS 122 for his constant support in every theatrical venture I've ever taken; Dave Lewis at Lower East Side Films; William Morris Agency, especially Scott Lambert, Brian Gersh, George Lane, Mike August, Clint Mitchell, James Dixon; my manager Tom Chestaro for coming in and tying all the knots; and last but the most important, all my supportive and forgiving friends who sat there through countless, indulgent readings and to the nameless fans who did the same—thanks y'all.

—John Leguizamo

Special thanks to: John Leguizamo, for everything, but especially for letting me rip painful memories out of his head like so many rotten teeth and then being OK about trying to make it funny. To Julie "Nappy" Merberg, who sacrificed many hours to my mistress, John Leguizamo, and whose support and

F
r
e
a
k
....

work are responsible for this book and so much else. Mom, Drew, Dad, Susan, Doug, Bisi, Jessica, Zach and my Nans for family stuff to draw upon; Will Potter, Todd Owens, John Watkins, Seth Burns, Michael Robin for politely laughing through the horror of early readings; to Fausto for the use of his name; Gregory Mosher, for passion and a desire to return to a 5/1 ratio; and Mary South, for making *Freak* a book and taking a leap of faith based on an early reading to a hostile crowd. Also Mark Russell at PS 122, for providing a nurturing space, Jonathan and Hillary Reinis at Theatre on the Square, David Lewis, Jason Sloane, Kathy DeMarco, Aury Wallington, and Gena Merberg for helping with too many things to list that made the show happen. Thanks!

—David Bar Katz

L
e
g
u i z
a
m
o

....

ix

FOREWORD

It was the spring of '95 and John and I had just come off of a year and a half of working on "House of Buggin'." We were sitting around my apartment when John innocently suggested that we do a stand-up comedy show, some kind of John Leguizamo-in-Concert-Richard-Pryoresque-Extravaganza that would be different from John's previous shows in that it wouldn't be overtly theatrical. John then said it would be "fun," as though it would be a break for us.

But as soon as the writing began, something horrible happened: real emotion raised its ugly head. Our writing sessions, which had initially just been made up of riffing on jokes, were turning into in-

L
e
g
u i z
a
m
o

. . . .

xi

depth psychoanalytic sessions. In my little office we were delving into all the love, sickness, and horror that are the grist of an ethnic person's life, and we were still just on me. My family life had exactly paralleled John's in every way (other than being Jewish, going to prep school, and not knowing how to pronounce "pollo"), so I had an intimate understanding of his emotional life: we both adored our grandmothers, were both Momma's boys, and both had a love/hate relationship with our fathers—we loved them, they hated us.

The first thing people always ask me after they see the show is, "Did it all really happen to John, is it all true?" (The exception being my mother who is now convinced that *my* father had me de-flowered at a Kentucky Fried Chicken.) To answer the truth question, I'll break down a couple of scenes in the play to give the reader an "insider's view."

There is a scene where John throws his own shit while playing in the pool at a Jewish resort. Now, John really did go to a Jewish resort as a child, though he did not actually throw shit there. But because he has thrown his own shit at other times in his life, I consider the story true.

There's also a scene where John is hit so hard he

F
r
e
a
k

dies—his soul leaves his body and ascends to heaven. Now, it is true that John has been hit (many times, actually). It is also true that his soul has left his body, but rather than ascending to heaven, as we've depicted it in *Freak,* his soul plunged down into a burning pit until it reached Hades, where it was greeted by Satan. I thought it best to edit this a bit. We don't want to scare the kids.

So there you have it; *Freak,* 100% kind-of-true.*

—David Bar Katz,
Lower East Side, June 19, 1997

*Or, as our lawyers insist we put it, the characters in *Freak* are wildly exaggerated for comic effect and bear little or no resemblance to actual people.

A NOTE FROM THE
AuTHOR

The following text is based on the stage show "Freak—A Semi-Demi-Quasi-Pseudo Autobiography." The show was written to be performed but has been adapted here to be a joyous read. Because we are right now in the midst of the show's developmental process, this version represents where the show is at this exact moment, June 19, 1997. It will be different tomorrow and even more different the day after. We only tell you this because if you try to read along with the book to a performance, you're gonna get real confused.

—**John Leguizamo & David Bar Katz**

L
e
g
u i z
a
m
o

· ·

x u

MEETING WOMB

I've changed my parents' names to Fausto and Lala, to protect the innocent, namely me. I was born in Latin America, 'cause my moms was there. And when I was born, my moms was in labor for 48 hours, but she didn't care because she was enthralled with the miracle of creating life. "Ow! Desgraciado, get this parasite out of me! Get it out of me now!! Coño."

I've changed my parents' names to Fausto and Lala, to protect the innocent, namely me. I was born in Latin America, 'cause my moms was there. And when I was born, my moms was in labor for forty-eight hours, but she didn't care because she was enthralled with the miracle of creating life. "Ow! Desgraciado, get this parasite out of me! Get it out of me now!! Coño."

And my dad's going, "If I had a nickel for every time I heard that."

The doctor was also a little anxious. "Push! Ms. Liquidzamo, Ms. Legs and amo, leg of lamb . . . Just push ma'am!"

"With what, cabrón! With what?!!"

And Dad says, "I'm paying you, doctor! Why don't you pull!?"

"I am pulling! He's a stubborn little fuck."

"Then leave him in there. Get up, woman, we're leaving."

"But Fausto, he's half out."

"So wear something loose. Come on, woman."

So they walked out and my first view of the world was upside down and between my moms' legs. And they wonder why I have problems.

*M*y parents left Latin America during the big plantain famine of the late sixties, and when they arrived in New York City they had such thick accents they couldn't even understand each other. My moms got all her English from watching television. "Fausto, chock full of nuts is the heavenly coffee, they're creepy and they're cookie, that . . . that . . . that's all folks!"

"Woman, what the hell did you just say?"

"How should I know? I'm speaking English."

At the airport, the nice, very white, very southern customs officer comes over to help. "Come now, strip naked! Deep cavity search time. Last week we found five Nicaraguans inside one of you people."

He starts searching my moms.

"OOhh, his hands are cold. Fausto, why don't you touch me like this?"

" 'Cause I'm not looking for anything. Hey, Mr. Officer, if we're being searched, why are you naked?"

"Shut up and bend over!"

He puts on a rubber glove and welcomes my dad to America.

"No, mister, please no! ow, ow, ow!" Then my dad started singing, "America America God shed his grace on thee."

The shuttle from the airport said "Miserable and Huddled Masses" and my pops is like, "This is our bus," so we jumped on and ended up in the present-day Ellis Island—Jackson Heights, Queens. Our tenement building was like the modern Tower of Babel. When I walked through the streets I'd see every ethnicity under the sun. The Hindi guy would be like, "You want curry candy? It burn the shit out of your buttocks. Ring of fire." Then the Jamaican rasta, "You people multiply like roaches go back, blood clots, batty fufu, chatty chatty. Tinga linga ling hear the money ring. Buyaca buyaca." And the Korean newsstand guy, "This is not a library, little punks. You buy magazine or kick your ass."

My parents worked twenty-eight hours a day, fourteen days a week. I'm not bad at math; it's just that Latin people have to make the most of their time. But my pops always took time out of his busy schedule to tell us his own version of an American bedtime story. "Once upon a time there was a Little Red Riding Hood and she went into the woods and got a green card and lived happily ever after. Now shut the fuck up and go to sleep!"

*O*f course, we Latin guys are always treated like little kings by our moms, and that's where we get that macho shit going to the max. And my moms would fill my head with it even when I was a baby in my high chair getting fed.

"You, you are the center of the universe. You are all things to me. Don't be tan estupid. Let the world come to you. Fuck everyone else, mi'jo, you are the prize—ah-ah, learn to share!" (Moms couldn't resist my strained carrots.)

"And remember, mi'jo, any woman that fucks you will probably fuck somebody else, okay? And you don't want to marry a whore! 'Cause no woman's good enough for my little Latin King."

At this point she would usually break down. I'd be like, "What's a whore, mommy?"

Slap! Right across my innocent chubby little face.

"Don't you ever repeat back to me what I say to you in the afternoons when I've been drinking a little."

Now, I have a theory that everybody's got a nice grandmother and a mean, evil, insane one. And I was always afraid that if they ever touched, their converse powers would mutually annihilate each other. I was eight when I first learned which was which. I was at a family barbecue with forty or fifty of my cousins carpooling on one hibachi. And my gramps was there on his life support system. We were keeping him alive against his will. Because my pops wanted him to live long enough so he would suffer what he had made my pops suffer. He would always motion me over, then he'd be like . . . "Pull the plug. No one's looking, John, pull the plug!"

"But, abuelito, you know I'm not supposed to touch your iron lung . . . "

"Just do it. Just do it. Mother@#$%*!"

"Okay. Goodbye, Gramps."

I'd give him a kiss, then pull the plug. But my dad had an uncanny ability to sense my grandfather escaping. He'd rush over just in time . . . "Hey, you know you're not supposed to put your grandfather out of his misery."

Then he'd plug him back in. "Nice try, old man."

I always tried to avoid my cousins Speedy and Boulevard, 'cause the games they played with the police by day, they reenacted on me by weekend. "Johnny, ven, mira, ven, quiero hablar contigo. Let's play police brutality. I'm a cop and tu eres un criminal. Aqui, take this gun!"

And they would toss a gun into my hand.

"I don't wanna play!" I'd scream. But it would be too late.

"Take him down, he's got a gun." Then they would jump on me and kick me and sing, "We're playing with Johnito, Johnito."

You might know my cousin Speedy—he's that shirtless Latin guy that you see on "Cops" each week. So I ran up to one of my grams for comfort. And my grandmother would cradle my little cherub face in her hands and say, "Ay, pobrecito, nenito consentido, what are you, a little girl? Come here, come here, let me put a dress on you, you little pussy!"

"I am what I eat." Grams' hand came flying up from

South America, across the Bronx, down Spanish Harlem, and smacked me in the face. "Ow! I read that somewhere. I hope your Miracle Ear breaks, you scrotum-faced old . . ."

"What did you say?" Grams hissed. "Like I care what a little fag thinks of me. Oh, look everyone, look at my little granddaughter. Speedy, Boulevard, come here, come here. I'll hold her down while you kick her ass."

And she was the *nice* Grandma. So then I ran up to my other grams, hoping for comfort, my midget Grama Dulce, which is Spanish for candy, 'cause her fingers were always sticky even though she never ate any candy. She was a Seventh-Day Adventist and had powerful beliefs, like, *The Exorcist* was actually a documentary, and that since there were no Latin people in *Star Trek* it was proof they weren't planning on having us around for the future. Her opinions got especially strong after she'd tip back a few fifths of holy water. Then she'd slip into this scary other voice and say things like, "If you (hiccup) levitate any furniture in my house or spit green puke on my clothes, I'm going to slap the shit out of you. And that goes for all one—two—of you."

Leguizamo

. . . .

9

"But Grama Dulce, I know it's not you, it's the alcohol talking," I'd insist.

"Lies! Lies!" she'd scream (hiccup). "You're the Prince of Lies. I know who you are, Lucifer. Leave the body of my grandson, demon!" Then she'd grab me and say, "Hold still. I'm going to drive your evil spirit away! Lord bless this Jack Daniel's." And she'd toss her drink in my face.

"It burns. My eyes. It burns," I'd cry out.

But Grams, she just says, " 'Cause you're wicked. Now let me finish the purge. Chango, mondongo, mofongo, bacalao. Chuleta, chancleta panti pa'-fuera."

I didn't wanna disappoint her; I knew this could be her last exorcism. So I'd start speaking in tongues and turning into Satan. I'd start jumping around and shaking and muttering in Hebrew and Arabic, Italian and ancient Chinese. Then I'd say, "I am Satan the cloven-hoofed. I've come to claim you as my wife. Come here, crusty old lady."

"Here I am, Satan—take me," Grams offered.

And then I'd have to remind her, "But it's just me, Grams. Your little Johnny."

She'd snap right out of it and slap me. "Don't you ever summon Satan again, cabroncito malcriado.

This is for Jesus *(slap!)* and this is for La Virgin Mary *(slap!)* and this is for making me miss happy hour!" *(slap! slap! slap!)*

"But Grama, it's only seven-thirty," I'd point out.

"Oh, good, I still have twenty minutes, then." And off she'd go.

L
e
g
u i z
a
m
o

THIRD WORLD LOGIC

Now our apartment was so puny it wished it were a project. It was a seventies nightmare; our walls were avocado green with brown linoleum and a nuclear orange shag rug; we were trying to re-create the papaya of our tropix and those seventies lamps that hung like an alien eyeball staring at us. And the centerpiece, the pièce de résistance of this mess, was our TV, my dad's pride and joy.

ow our apartment was so puny it wished it were a project. It was a seventies nightmare; our walls were avocado green with brown linoleum and a nuclear orange shag rug; we were trying to re-create the papaya of our tropix and those seventies lamps that hung like an alien eyeball staring at us. And the centerpiece, the pièce de résistance of this mess, was our TV, my dad's pride and joy. It was sacred to him, because my pops could Latinize everybody in America; we would let the screen get real dusty so that everybody looked nice and dark and Spanish. And my father was the only one allowed to watch TV, 'cause he thought the more you watch it, the more you wear it out. Dad was operating under some kind of third-world logic.

He'd say, "Don't use my television and don't sit on my furniture unless we have important guests. Use the floor for sitting and the kitchen sink for eating. And we're not gonna buy any more food if you keep eating it! Food, I repeat, is for the guests and the animals. And I just brushed the dogs, so don't pet 'em! And get the hell off the rug, I just vacuumed it. And stop sucking up all my oxygen—I'm breathing it."

My brother and I would be like, "Okay, Dad, okay."

I was a prisoner in my own house. I felt like . . . Anne Frank. Except she only had Nazis to deal with. And every time my father had something important to say, the subway would go by. And it wouldn't have been a problem, but we shared a wall with the number 7 Train.

He'd start lecturing us, "I'm only gonna say this once. The most important thing I want you to do is . . ." and sure enough the train would roar by, drowning him out " . . . or I'm gonna kick your ass!"

Paralyzed with fear, I'd say, "Okay, Dad—no problem."

But as soon as my father was out of the house, my brother Poochie and I would be like a Navy SEAL operation. "Now, Poochie," I'd say, "it's 1800 hours, and the *Prince of Darkness* will be . . ."

Poochie freaked out. "Prince of Darkness? You didn't tell me nuttin' about no Prince of Darkness. Na-ah, I'm not listening. Mamaku mamasa mama mamakusa . . ." He put his hands over his ears and closed his eyes.

"Poochie," I'd have to yell, "the Prince of Darkness is the man you know as Dad. Now you go put the bubble wrap under the rug so when Dad comes through the hall we'll hear him. Now we're punishment-proof. We outsmarteded that ignor-anus! What a maroon! What a sucker-butt! Ha ha! *Ungawa ungawa, Dad's away for two hours. A beep beep, we're TV freaks. Get stupid.* Poochie, turn the TV on." Then we'd settle down for a TV frenzy—"Spiderman," "Underdog," "Gigantor" the space robot. Everything

F
r
e
a
k

16

was great until I messed with the antenna. I'd be swinging around in time to the "Spiderman" theme when suddenly . . . SNAP! The blood drained out of my body and into the ground and back to Latin America. "Poochie, I broke the antenna!"

And just then, "John!" Luckily, it was just my moms.

"Mom. Why are you climbing in through the window?" I wondered.

"The rent is due. What the hell are you doing? You're sitting on the furnitura. You're eating the food. Ay, dios mio, you broke the antenna!! Oh my God! I'm looking into the face of a dead boy." Moms had a knack for calming me down.

"Mom, use me for cruel animal experimentation, sell me to child pornographers, but don't let him get his hands on me!!!" I begged, throwing myself around her legs.

"No, don't, don't. I'll miss you. But now I must distance myself," she said. "Come, Poochie, you're an only child now. Ciao. Get off me, John. Get off."

Then all of a sudden we hear the sound of snapping bubble wrap and Pop's voice, cursing, "Coño, qué es toda esta mierda de bubble wrap, hijo de puta."

Leguizamo

17

So I'm blowing and fanning the TV, 'cause my pops would feel it for heat. And my moms goes into rescue mode, "I'll take care of your father," she whispered to me as Pops came in. "Fausto, you look so ultra sexy. You look so sexy. Yes, you do. Let's have a game of one-on-one?" Moms flashed a breast at my father, pulling out all the stops. "You and me. One-on-one."

But my father wasn't taking the bait. "Woman, put that nipple away. I just wanna watch my television. C'mon fellas."

My moms tried another approach. "Good, good. Okay, then, why don't you go downstairs and play pool. Hmm? Okay? Play some pool?"

God bless my moms. We didn't have a downstairs.

Pops turned on the TV. "I said no, woman. What the hell's all that static. I can't tell Sonny from Cher."

"I'll fix it! I'll fix it!" I offered, right away. So I moved the good piece of antenna for all I was worth. "Like this, Dad? Or this? Here?"

"Move the other one!" Pops barked.

So I pretended to move the broken antenna. *Trompe l'oeil.* I frantically shifted my body around while holding the broken antenna in place. "There?

Like so? Perfect?" I was using up all my available cuteness.

"Move away from that television," Pops ordered.

"Okay, I am away," I said, inching over a bit.

"Get the hell out of the room, you little shit!" Pops yelled. I stayed in the same place but moon-walked.

"Okay, I'm leaving the room, the neighborhood . . ." and as I head for the door, I trip. He sees the antenna came off in my hand. "It's a spear and I'm a hunter?" I offer meekly. I know what's coming next.

My pops field-goals me with a kick across the room. Luckily the nice hard brick wall broke my fall. And my head opened up like a piñata. "Dad, look at the pretty candy," I cooed. Then everything went black. And as I was waiting to die, my life started flashing before me. Yachting on the Cape, debutante orgies at Vassar, Monet sunsets on the Riviera. Wait a minute—that's not my life. And I felt my soul leave my body and hover over, and I looked down and— "damn, why didn't anybody tell me I had such a flat face," and I sailed out the window toward the light higher and higher, and I remembered my comix and how Spiderman once said to Ironman, "That to escape the pain, one must move toward the pain." And

L
e
g
u i z
a
m
o

19

my soul thought, "Fuck that noise!" and sprinted the hell outta the house, and into the sky . . . and as I flew closer to the light, I saw a divine being, a beautiful woman standing there naked, her pert breasts glistening in the moon beams, and I wanted to suckle the breasts of all nurturing unconditional loves, and her arms were outstretched, beckoning me toward her . . . and just when I was about to touch her, I caught a whiff of my favorite Chino Latino restaurant, shrimp fried rice and platano maduro, and suddenly I wanted to live. If only for the plantanos, I wanted to live and *boom,* I was back in my body with all this new-found wisdom. The first words out of my mouth said it all:

"Poochie broke the antenna."

Poor, slow, chubby Poochie. I watched him go off screaming and yelling, "No! Don't! Anything but that. I'm your favorite. Remember, Dad?" And I just stood there watching, the only brother I had, beaten senseless with the antenna, and all I could think was, "Thank God it's not me." But I don't wanna leave you with a bad impression of my pops. 'Cause he wasn't always this brutal. No, sometimes he drank, too.

DAD

DRUNK

And when my pops drank he became the most loveable son of a bitch in the land. And he'd go out on the fire escape and he'd sit me on his knee and he'd start with the hugs and the playful teasing and he'd start wailing to old-world songs.

And when my pops drank he became the most loveable son of a bitch in the land. And he'd go out on the fire escape and he'd sit me on his knee and he'd start with the hugs and the playful teasing and he'd start wailing to old-world songs.

"Vivo solo sin tí/Sin poderte

olvidar/Un momento no más/Vivo pobre de amor/A la espera de quién/No me dá una ilusión/Miro el tiempo pasar/Y al infierno llegar/Todos menos a tí/Si otro amor me viniera a llamar no lo quiero ni oir . . . oir . . ." He trailed off when he forgot the lyrics. "I proposed to your mother with this song; boy, was she easy. Having a good time? You enjoying this? Good, 'cause I'm gonna take it all away from you. Then you'll really know how miserable life can be. You know, it's time you start providing for this family."

"But I'm only ten, Pops."

"Oh, so now it's time to sit back and rest on your laurels, Mr. Big Shot? C'mere, I love you. What are you cringing at? Afraid of a little affection? I'm your father, you little faggot. Come on, give me a kiss. You kiss me or I'll punch the shit out of you."

"Okay, Dad." I went along with it and kissed him.

"Not on the lips, you little freak! You're so lucky to have a dad like me who comes home at all, when I could be out fucking hot, stinking women and having a great time, but am I doing that? No, because I'm right here spending quality time with my loser of a son." Then Pops would whistle for my mom. "Hey, woman, bring your big fat ass over here, I wanna look at it. Can you believe you were squeezed out of those two butt cheeks? Mmm. But it's home." Then he'd try to get me to drink a little. "Come on, you punk, have a shot. C'mon, it's just happy juice."

But I wouldn't touch the stuff. "Na-ah, it tastes like dookie. Dad, why don't you just quit drinkin'?"

" 'Cause I'm not a quitter. Drink it," he said, "and I'll give you ten bucks."

"Deal! But let me see the money first. Oh, okay. I trust you." I took a swallow. "Euw. That's good. Now where's my money?"

"Where's *my* money not to tell your mother you're a little alcoholic?" Pops asked.

I called out for Moms right away.

"Who do you think your mother's gonna believe—me or your Cuervo breath?" Pops pointed out.

He had a point. I gave in. "I'll have another round." My head started spinning. "I love you, Dad. I really do."

"That's my boy," he said, watching me take another pull on the bottle. "That's why I'm gonna tell you my secret scheme. And if you tell anybody, I'll have to kill you. Bobo pendejo, I'm gonna rent every room in this apartment till I own the building, the block. I'm gonna be King of Tenements, the Latino Donaldo Trumpo. I'm gonna elevate my situation, I'm gonna

F

r

e

a

k

26

be an entrepreneurial business man, not a servant. 'Cause a servant serves and I don't want to serve."

" 'Cause my dad's no servant," I yelled, clinking glasses with him.

"All right, calm down. Someday you're gonna be the Crowned Prince of Tenements, Johnito."

"You're a regular genius, Dad. I'm so glad we could be this close. I always pictured it like this. You and me and the stink of alcohol. Dad, I got a secret too." I took another sip to steady myself. "It was me who broke the antenna. See, I knew you'd understand." I made a scramble for the window, but Pops grabbed my leg and pulled me back out to the fire escape. "Dad! No, Dad! Mom! It was really Poochie, like I said the first time. No! Dad, don't!"

Those were some of the best times I had with my father, but of course with the onslaught of puberty, I quickly realized I could have a much better time alone.

THE
FIRST
ORGASM

I was about twelve the first time I tried to masturbate. "Ahh," I thought I broke it, 'cause something that wasn't pee actually leaked out and I was like, "Ahh." I actually thought I spilled the glue that kept it together. But it felt so good that pretty soon I was becoming unglued every chance I got. About ten times a day and experimenting. I wanted to feel the whole world through my penis.

was about twelve the first time I tried to masturbate. I thought I broke it, 'cause something that wasn't pee actually leaked out and I was like, "Ahh!" I actually thought I spilled the glue that kept it together. But it felt so good that pretty soon I was becoming unglued every chance I got. About ten times a day and experiment-ing. I wanted to feel the whole world through my penis. "I wonder what it would feel like if I touch a sandwich with my penis? Ooh, mayonaisey. What if I touch it to glass? Ooh, cold! My dog?" (You're sick—I know what you're thinking.)

I could play with it all day long. "Arise, Sir Loin-of-beef," I said, tapping an imaginary subject with my newly found "sword." "Now let me see if I can lift this chair with the phone book, the radio, and the shoes on it. Okay, maybe just the chair. Okay, how about just a tie? Aha! Success! Damn, I'm a mon-ster. Don't be frightened." I tied a Windsor knot in the tie. "Now I'm ready for company." Then I would begin the fun part. "Okay, let me see if I can hit that Kristy McNichol poster, bounce and strike my Six-Million-Dollar-Man action figure, then hit Grams' blood-pressure medicine, and ricochet into the toilet. My load d'amour finally landed. Oops, my brother's toothbrush. Oh well, he never uses it anyhow."

Out of nowhere, my pops is at the door. "Come on, you little punk. You're not doing what I think you're doing, are you? Not in my house, you don't!"

"No! Leave me alone! I'm going mad," I shouted

through the door as I continued to ferociously masturbate.

But my kid brother, Poochie, whom I renamed "the
boy called bitch," decides to be all helpful. "I'll let
you in, Dad. I know how to open the door, Dad. Blame
the antenna on me, will he?" I heard him mutter to
himself.

The door kicks open and my whole family rushes
into the bathroom, and there I am, totally naked,
perched on the sink and my moms goes, "You are
dead to me! I can't look." But then she peeks, appre-
ciatively. "Ay, John!"

"What the hell are you doing in here?" my dad
yells.

I think fast. "See, I was about to take a shower
when I decided . . . I needed . . . to . . . change the light
bulb."

"With your erect penis?" he asks.

"Um . . . I couldn't reach with my hands?" I try,
hopefully.

"And why are your moms' panties on your head?"
he continues.

"I couldn't find my shower cap?" I try, again.

"What's this *goo* on my toothbrush, John?"
Poochie asks.

"That's my . . . new toothpaste?"

Dad says, "Then prove it! Brush your teeth. Now."

"But . . . but . . . I don't wanna brush my teeth! Grama . . . please!" I start to beg.

"I'm not touching that cum," Grams states.

And that was the dental-hygiene crossroads for my family, 'cause no one really ever brushed with confidence again.

L
e
g
u i z
a
m
o

FELLAS ON SEX

...would be huddled together sharing misinformation about the secrets of sex. Where the homies would be on one side and the homettes on the other. And my crew of inner-city misfits would be going to house parties. So my father put a glass door on the bathroom, so I was forced to look elsewhere for my sexual exploration. And luckily about that time we started going to house parties.

So my father put a glass door on the bathroom, so I was forced to look elsewhere for my sexual exploration. And luckily about that time we started going to house parties. Where the homies would be on one side and the homettes on the other. And my crew of inner-city mis-

fits would be huddled together sharing misinformation about the secrets of sex.

My friend Bobo said, "Yo, you have to pork a girl as
fast as you can or it'll close up on you and lock up on
your wood. And there's a bitch attached to you wher-
ever you go and what not. I'm serious. No joke, kid."

Then Lollipop offered his wisdom. "Yo, a wet
dream can be dangerous if you sleep with an electric
blanket. Word 'em up."

My friend Xerox, he's dancing around, and he says,
"Yo, pulling on your dick makes it biggerer. Not that
I need to know this info—this is for ya'lls benefit. You
know what I'm saying, John?"

So, I've got to hop in and show 'em I know what's
what. "A menstrual cycle has . . . three wheels."

"Yeah, whatever, John," Bobo says. "Yo, let's have
a 'who dick bigger' contest. My dick is five fingers
plus a small X-men Wolverine action figure. Ha ha."

Xerox says, "Dag, mine's the size of a Devil Dog
with the end bit off. Ha ha. You know what I'm sayin'."

So I say, "Mine's like a can of tuna," and they look
at me weird til I continue, " 'cause you know it's the
width that counts!"

FRESH-
AIR
FUNK

I was a very misunderstood child. So my parents finally got sick of my friends' influence on me and my strange sexual blatherings and signed me up with the Fresh-Air Fund for the summer. That's where they take a poor underprivileged disenfranchised kid and have him stay with a rich New England family. They expand your horizons, show you how great and fun life can be, and then just when you're getting comfortable—three meals a day, lead-free paint chips—they snatch it all away. So if you didn't know how poor you were, **now your ass really knows!**

I was a very misunder-
stood child. So my parents finally got sick of my friends'
influence on me and my strange
sexual blatherings and signed
me up with the Fresh-Air Fund
for the summer. That's where
they take a poor underprivileged
disenfranchised kid and have

him stay with a rich New England family. They expand your horizons, show you how great and fun life can be, and then just when you're getting comfortable—three meals a day, lead-free paint chips—they snatch it all away. So if you didn't know how poor you were, now your ass really knows!

There was one horrible thing that the Fresh-Air Fund faculty hadn't prepared me for: men born in this country don't have foreskins. I thought everybody was like me until I walked in on my Fresh-Air brother. It was in one of those outdoor showers that I saw my first circumcised penis.

"Oh, dag. What's wrong with you?" I asked. "You're a mutilated mutant, you silly little freak."

And then my other Fresh-Air brother walks in and he has the same deformity.

"What's wrong with you people?" I asked.

Then the father comes in and he's scarred, too.

"Oh, my God, it's a colony of mutants. It must be the water. You're mutants. Mutants. Weirdos."

But then my Fresh-Air Fund brother says, "Father, what's wrong with him? Look at all that skin."

And the other brother chimes in, "It looks like a slug."

"No, no," disagrees the first brother. "I think it looks like a mouse in a garden hose."

"Now, now. Don't make fun, boys," scolds the Fresh-Air-Fund father. "Little John comes from a primitive land where they don't have the benefits of running water and surgery. If your grades aren't good and you're disobedient and you don't get into the Ivy League, your foreskins will grow back and eventually cover your face, skin, and body, and possibly even your loved ones."

But all I can say is, "You don't like it? It's my anteater. It's a protective covering not unlike a turtleneck."

I thought it was a conspiracy. Why didn't anybody tell me? For years after that I showered in my jeans—'cause you never know. But back in the city I wasn't afraid to show my penis, 'cause everybody's was like mine, just bigger.

Every evening in my Fresh-Air-Fund household, we'd gather around a roaring fire. I don't know why. It was summertime . . . And my Fresh-Air-Fund father would hold forth. "You see, little brown man, people of good breeding sip cognacs and talk about lacrosse, and pet their golden retrievers." He took a big puff on his pipe. "I think I'll forego all social activities tonight. Goodnight, little inner-city foundling. Let's go upstairs, honey-bunny; I feel f-r-i-s-k-y."

Like I don't know how to spell *fry-sky.* I knew they were about to sex up. And I ran and hid under their bed, hoping for some wild adult porn. But all I heard were these real quiet squeaks.

Then my Fresh-Air-Fund father says, "Oh, oh, thank you, dear." And my Fresh-Air-Fund mother says, "No, let's not make it worse by talking. Good-night."

Now it was a whole 'nother ball game at my aunt Anissette's up in Spanish Harlem with her and her lover/mechanic guy, and they'd be, like . . . "Take this and that and some of this. Take it all, you whore, you slut, you bitch."

And then he would say, "I know I can't never truly satisfy you, but at least I fuck you, right?"

And my aunt Anissette would yell, "Wrong! No, you don't fuck me, I fucks you. A'right? And you call that fucking? I didn't even know you was in the room. Ay, please!"

L
e
g
u i z
a
m
o

. . . .

43

JEWISH RESORT

By the end of that summer, my pops' tenement scheme had finally paid off. And when I got back from the Fresh-Air Fund I hardly recognized him. He became Nuyorican rich, which meant he started wearing fake fur coats and fake gold chains. He was a cross between Huggy Bear and Mr. Roper. Since Dad had now "made it," he wanted to join a fancy country club, but the WASPs said, "No fucking way."

By the end of that summer, my pops' tenement scheme had finally paid off. And when I got back from the Fresh-Air Fund I hardly recognized him. He became Nuyorican rich, which meant he started wearing fake fur coats and fake gold chains. He was a cross between Huggy

Bear and Mr. Roper. Since Dad had now "made it," he wanted to join a fancy country club, but the WASPs said, "No fucking way." So we went to the second-best thing: a Jewish country club, and we got in because of a little white lie.

Our waiter would greet us, "Ah, are you the rich Leguizam-bergs of Jackson Heights? Well, your table is right here. Beware the pogroms. It'll start all over again, but you with such a lovely family. And, kine-ahora, who are these lovely children? You little bubbala. You must be kvelling. Their names?"

My pops, in his fur coat and chains, thought fast. "This is . . . Abraham. This is Moses. Say thank you, Abraham!"

"Thank you," I said. But Pops said, "Smile." I smiled. "More Jewish," he said. I smiled wider.

And a few weeks into the summer, disaster struck—over the P.A. system, loud as can be, came an announcement: "Would Mr. Leguizam-berg go to the front desk, immediately."

And my dad marched—all self-righteous— fronting like he'd won a mahjong set, with his fake fur coat flowing behind him.

The manager was buffing his nails, waiting. "Mr.

L
e
g
u i z
a
m
o

. . . .

47

Leguizam-berg. We have a very nice resort that caters to a certain . . . classy clientele and they expect a certain courtesy . . ."

"And your point is?" my dad interrupted.

"Your children are—how can I put this delicately?—foul-mouthed primitives . . . and they shit in the pool."

"And?" Pops prompted.

"Well, then they started to throw it at each other."

"So?" Pops was patiently waiting for the point.

"They were throwing their own shit!" The manager yelled.

My pops just shrugged. "It's what kids do. You throw some to a friend, and he throws it back to you. Throwing shit is part of a happy childhood."

Then all of a sudden my cousin Speedy appeared in the doorway. "Your house got on fire and completely burned down. Grama Dulce fell asleep with a cigar in her mouth," Speedy gasped.

My pops was silent, stunned. Then he got all choked up. "Look at my kids down there. So innocent and young . . . throwing their own shit. Not knowing what they lost. Why me, God? Why me? Always out to get the littlest guy, always fucking over the humble. Here, you wanna fuck somebody? You

F

r

e

a

k

. . . .

48

wanna do somebody up the anus, God? Here, take Speedy."

Now, I don't know if it was the loss of his tenement, the loss of his standing in the Jewish community, or the way he talked to God, but he couldn't take it no more, and was arrested in a nearby mall, naked, stealing pennies out of the fountain and claiming he was invisible. And my moms was all upset. "Children, don't look. Officer, is there anything you can do?"

But Pops barged right in. "Do? There's nothing he can do. Because I'm invisible. What's causing that mysterious splashing? What strange power is causing your pants to fall down unexpectedly, breaking all the laws of space and time? 'Tis I—the *invisible* Tenement King."

After my dad undid that cop's pants—he became the *unconscious* invisible Tenement King.

SURRO-GATE MOMS

And since my moms was working so much, my uncle Sanny became our **surrogate moms.** We couldn't afford the chicken. When they came out with Shake 'n Bake Barbecue, it was a fucking national holiday in my house. And times were tight—every day of every month we ate Shake 'n Bake. Right out of the box. With Dad unavailable, my moms had to take up the slack.

With Dad unavailable, my moms had to take up the slack. And times were tight—every day of every month we ate Shake 'n Bake. Right out of the box. We couldn't afford the chicken. When they came out with Shake 'n Bake Barbecue, it was a fucking national holiday in my house. And since my moms was working so much, my uncle Sanny became our surrogate moms. Now, my uncle Sanny was a little unconventional. He was what you'd call a triple threat: Latin, gay, and deaf. And he was so wise he was dubbed the Einstein of Jackson Heights.

"Ay, fo," Sanny exclaimed. "I know things even God doesn't know! Ay, puta, que escándalo, me jodí. At Christmas I always made a lousy Santa. Instead of filling the stockings, I was always trying them on, Ay, fo! Poof, bad thoughts be gone. Ay, que escándalo, me jodí, la loca dame huevo."

I loved him and I told him so. "I wanna grow up and be just like you, uncle Sanny, except for the liking men part."

"I know your father doesn't respect me," Sanny said, "but that's bullshit. Because feature this: many highly respectable individuals of ancient and modern times have been homosexuals: Plato, Michelangelo, Disney. Oops, I outed him. Que escándalo, lo jodí."

Just 'cause we were poor didn't mean we didn't get culture. 'Cause one day my uncle Sanny took us to Broadway, The Great White Way. He finessed this technique he coined "Second acting." First we mixed in with the intermission smokers and then we tried to slip into the theater undetected to catch the second act.

"John, Poochie, here, smoke these," Uncle Sanny said. "Uh-uh-uh, Menthol for you, Poochie. You're only twelve. No, they're not children, they're midgets."

So with stolen programs in hand we waited for everyone to sit down, then we ran down the aisles and grabbed the empty seats.

I wasn't sitting with anyone I knew and I'm ascared of being clocked and I'm peeping at this ridiculous musical *Chorus Line* thing when I hear somebody called Morales on stage. There was a Latin person in the show. And she didn't have a gun or hypodermic needle in her hand and she wasn't a hooker or a maid and she wasn't servicing anybody so it was hard to tell if she was Latin and everybody's respecting her and admiring her . . . I was lost in this amazing moment, singing along as loud as I could. Then I felt a hand grab me and I was yanked up out of my seat by one of those Pilgrim ladies and beat with the flashlight. My brother got caught, too, 'cause he was still smoking his Kools, and Sanny

F
r
e
a
k

got busted, 'cause he was lip-syncing along too loudly. And I'm still like, "She's singing to me, she's singing to me!" And Uncle Sanny's yelling, "Shut the hell up and run! Run!" And that's how I got culture.

FRENCH
PASSING
-NOT!

Meanwhile my pops was scheming it. To keep food on the table he finally hit with the luck of the Latin and got a job as the headwaiter at the top French restaurant in Manny Hanny. And my brother Poochie's birthday came around and I thought I would give him an extra nice surprise and take him to Dad's restaurant. So we put on our best leisure suits and **subwayed it into Manhattan.**

eanwhile my pops was schememing it. To keep food on the table he finally hit with the luck of the Latin and got a job as the headwaiter at the top French restaurant in Manny Hanny. And my brother Poochie's birthday came around and I thought I would give him an extra nice surprise and take him to Dad's restaurant. So we put on our best leisure suits and subwayed it into Manhattan.

"John, we're not supposed to be in here. Dad's gonna open up a can of kick ass on us," Poochie worried.

"This is a birthday surprise for you and Dad, fat boy."

"I don't want to be called fat boy no more, John, I'm a man now."

"Okay, fat man," I conceded.

The waiter talked like he smelled something bad. "Bonjour. What will you be having, young sirs?"

"No offense, Mr. garçon, sir, but we'd like to be served by the *head*waiter, Mr. Leguizamo," I insisted.

"I'm not sure I'm familiar with that name," our waiter drawled.

"You must be new here, 'cause our dad runs this place. Why don't you make yourself useful and go find him, mister man, sir." I rolled my eyes at Poochie. "The help."

And I'm looking around for Dad and looking and I can't see him anywhere and he doesn't show up and there's only so much olive oil we could drink. And the kitchen doors swing open long enough so I can see a guy that looks a lot like my dad, but I know it can't be him, 'cause that guy's bending over a sink washing dishes. But then they swing open again. I look real closely. We had to get outta there.

I yank Poochie's leg. "Come on, Poochie. All of sudden I'm not in the mood for French. The sauces are too rich. I'm afraid I'll get male breasts. Let's get a pizza."

But Poochie pouts. "I'm not leaving till I see Dad order somebody around, John."

"You see that at home all the time. Every day. Now come on, Poochie, let's go, little man." I pull him toward the door.

"John, you ruined my birthday. I'll take pizza, but it better be large and no anchovies on my pizza. You think one of my legs is longerer than the other? John, why aren't you talking to me?" I was quiet as Poochie rambled on.

BLACK
IRISH

So I was an angry, disillusioned kid. And then we upgraded to a poor all-Irish neighborhood in Sunnyside, Queens, where we were the first Latin family, so we were like pioneers. Manifest destiny in reverse. And I see this real hot Irish chick. You know the type—red-headed, freckled, drunk, lapsed Catholic whore, ready to be inseminated by a wily Latin stud. Okay, I'm bitter—**they never liked me.**

So I was an angry, disillu-sioned kid. And then we up-graded to a poor all-Irish neighborhood in Sunnyside, Queens, where we were the first Latin family, so we were like pi-oneers. Manifest destiny in re-verse. And I see this real hot Irish chick. You know the type—

red-headed, freckled, drunk, lapsed Catholic whore, ready to be inseminated by a wily Latin stud. Okay, I'm bitter—they never liked me. So I'm having some green beer, and since everybody's Irish on St. Patrick's Day I figured I'll try out my gift and river-dance over to her, and I talk to her in the thickest Irish accent I can manage.

"Toy, hello, lassie, how's the Emerald Isle? You ever fuck a leprechaun? Erin go bragh and begorrah. Why are you looking at me like that? Is my shillelagh hanging out? Are my shenanigans banging about out?"

She took a long draw on her cigarette and said, "You don't look Irish to me."

"Oh, but I am, black Irish." I lifted my beer. "I'm parched above, lassie. Are you moist below?"

Okay, so I didn't say that. I said how much I respect Irish culture and what contributions they've made: U2, whiskey, cops, and, of course, Scotty. "Captain, the dilithium crystals are breaking up, the engine she's gonna blow. The heath the moor you know you got to go see *Trainspotting, Braveheart.* You sit through the whole movie and you can't understand a word even if you see it forty times."

"What kind of fucking moron are you?" she asked.

"Scotty's Scottish, asshole. Everybody knows that. Brian, Sean, Blarney, this Spanish guy is bothering me."

Then ten or fifteen of her hooligan brothers circled me, proof that the rhythm method doesn't work in the Irish community. We Latin people, we have rhythm, but we save it for dancing.

"Are you trying to get with our sister, you dirty Puerto Rican?" asked the biggest Irish brother.

"Well, your mother was booked, now wasn't she?" I remarked.

"I'll wipe up the street with ya, you little wetback!" He took a threatening step in my direction.

"But where, laddie? Where's the lad with the moist back?" I cried out, looking all around the bar. "I'll give him a taste of me fisticuffs. Where's the little fucker? I'll find the little fucker and get him for you."

"You! You're the lying little spic!" He wasn't fooled.

I was outnumbered, but I didn't care. I did what any proud Latin kid raised in the ghetto would do in that situation, and I make no apologies. I—acted like a retard. "I didn't touch the pretty lady, no I didn't. I gotta pee. Hold it for me. Why won't you hold it for me? It burns. Come on, blow on it. Why won't you blow on it?"

GUIDO-RAMA

So we had to move to Corona, which was an all-Italian neighborhood, so I was excited to be welcomed by our fellow swarthy, olive-skinned Mediterranean brothers and sisters. "Mira, oye, grazie prego, Pacino De Niro." My new Italian friend responded warmly, "You spic. You dumb fucking ugly dumb dumb fucking ugly dumb dumb ugly fucking dumb dumb dumb...Hey, Joey, did I use up dumb already?"

So we had to move, to Corona, which was an all-Italian neighborhood, so I was excited to be welcomed by our fellow swarthy, olive-skinned Mediterranean brothers and sisters. "Mira, oye, grazie prego, Pacino, De Niro."

My new Italian friend responded warmly. "You spic. You dumb fucking ugly dumb dumb fucking ugly dumb dumb ugly fucking dumb dumb dumb . . . Hey, Joey, did I use up dumb already?"

"Yeah, Ant-knee. Try . . . douchebag?"

"Yeah, you douchebag douchebag fucking bobouchebag bananafana fo fucking fouchebag fe fi fo mo mouchebag fucking douchebag forget about it. Youse douchebags ruined this neighborhood. Before youse came here there were nice houses and great stores, no doubt about it."

"Yeah, yeah, I know; we Latin people are the bacteria of the universe," I admitted. "We're lazy, we fuck too much, and look what I bought with my welfare check—a Guido joke book! And to think I almost wasted it on crack. Here's one I'm sure you'll like. How can you tell if your baby's a Guido? Give up? He won't use a pacifier unless it's got hair on it. That means that your mother has hair on her nipples. I like that one. That shit can't be true. You're the Guido, you tell me. Oh, shit, ha, ha, ha. Why aren't you laughing?"

They started stomping me and yoking me. So I did what any Latin kid would do in that situation—I acted like a retard again. "I gotta pee. Will you hold it for me?"

Unfortunately, they knew my Irish friends. "Hey, this is the clown the Irish Mic warned us about. You fucking bozo, I got a retarded brother. Give me my homey-be-good stick."

He started swinging at me so I tried another strategy. "Ow, ow. Yo, wait up . . . wait up fellas. I have . . . Tourette's. I have no control over what I say—it's completely involuntary, it just comes out, you fucking moron piece of white trash suck my long brown dick and like it like your mother does," I barked, and twitched and jerked around for effect. "I'm sorry. I'm really sorry. I don't know what came over me, saying that about your mother liking my dick and all, it's the Tourette's."

They bought it. "Oh, wow, it's horrible. Is there a cure for torres?"

"No, it's terminal and extremely contagious." Then I breathed on them. "Can I hang out with you guys?" They ran off.

FIRST LOVE—BLACK VENUS

She was my ebony princess, my Nubian bucket of love, **my Africanus romanticus.** Don't waste them. Now pull the plug." I knew she was going to be the first one. my Nubian bucket of love, John, you have three loves in your life. and the Italians hated me, I finally found a girl who loved me, and my grandfather said to me, "So we had to move again. Now as much as the Irish

So we had to move again. Now as much as the Irish and the Italians hated me, I finally found a girl who loved me, and my grandfather said to me, "John, you have three loves in your life. Don't waste them. Now pull the plug." I knew she was going to be the first one. She

F
r
e
a
k

was my ebony princess, my Nubian bucket of love, my Africanus romanticus. She was black and her pops was a Black Muslim, so when it finally came time to meet him, I thought, "This guy might be my future father-in-law." I came over in my best Elijah Muhammad bow tie and said, as nerdily as I could, "Hello sir, I'm here to pick your daughter up for a date."

Her black pops met me at the door, sucking on his teeth and popping out his cheek. "You don't fool me, boy. You don't look like a Muslim with that bow tie— you look like Pee-Wee Herman, and when I look at your white skin I wanna kill you."

"But I'm not white sir, I'm a Latino."

"Well, then I definitely don't wanna get caught up in an illegal-alien Mexican situation. I heard about you Mexicans, buying up all the Cabbage Patch dolls just to get the birth certificates," he said.

So I would have to sneak up to her window at night to avoid her pops, and I'd stand there and profess my undying love. "I love you, Yashica."

"What did you say?!" she yelled.

She lived on the fifty-eighth floor.

"I'll love you forever!!" I screamed again.

Then the neighbors called out, "Yeah, we love you,

too—now shut the fuck up and go to sleep." So she met me at the service elevator, then snuck me into her room. And it was so romantic—we put on some Al Green, she turned on the black light, we took off article after article of clothing till we were in our underwear only and I was about to finally lose my virginity. I looked at my beautiful black Venus. She looked at me.

Then she said, "Oh, my God, you are the whitetest motherfucker I ever saw. You glow in the dark."

"I love you, Yashica," I responded.

"Yeah, whatever. You don't get it, Translucent Man. Oh, my God—turn around for a second. I can see your intestines, like a guppy. I can tell what you had for lunch. Hold on, hold on, I want my sister to see your blue veiny ass, guppy boy. Shanté. Shanté, come here, girl."

KENTUCKY FRIED DE-VIRGIN-IZING

So I was still a virgin. So for my sixteenth birthday, Dad, seeing his son's miserably failed attempts at becoming a man, decided to give nature a little push. He got the car out and loaded us in. "Hey, John, Poochie, get in back. John, you know since the average pinga is six inches and the average vaginga is eight inches, there are two miles of unused vaginga in New York City and I'm gonna find some for you. Okay, here we are. **Poochie, wait in the car.**"

So I was still a virgin. So for my sixteenth birthday, Dad, seeing his son's miserably failed attempts at becoming a man, decided to give nature a little push.

He got the car out and loaded us in. "Hey, John, Poochie, get in back." My dad suddenly got serious. "John, you know since the average pinga is six inches and the average vaginga is eight inches, there are two miles of unused vaginga in New York City and I'm gonna find some for you. Okay, here we are. Poochie, wait in the car."

"Kentucky Fried Chicken. How's the Colonel gonna make me a man?" I wondered.

"Not the Colonel, stupid. It's a lady who works here. She fries/batters chickens by day and chokes chickens by night."

And the next thing I know I'm in the back of the Kentucky Fried Chicken and this mad, fine, stout German lady in her late forties comes out. "Your swarthy looks are so dark and I feel sorry for you, so I will fuck you. I'll think of it as war reparations."

So she has me over the fryer and we're sucking face. Then she reaches down and touches my Thing. It was the first time someone other than me had touched it, so as you can imagine, my Thing's buggin' out.

I can hear it talking to me. "Uh, Johnny, what's she doing?"

"Just relax. We're getting some," I try to reassure my Thing.

"Um, she's being a little rough—she's pulling, Johnny!"

"She's German. Now will you shut up?!!"

My Thing is not giving up. "Johnny, can't you just do it? I like how you do it. You know where to touch, what I like . . . What I need . . . "

Then she put the whole thing in her mouth.

Suddenly, my Thing is singing a different tune. "Ooh! Why didn't you ever do this?"

I told him, "I couldn't reach!"

Now, you know how people always say that time distorts memory. Details change. Exaggeration occurs with the retelling. But not in this case. Before I could think, she'd stripped down and put my hand on her little vertical smile. Her coochie was a failed experiment from *The Island of Dr. Moreau.* Now, I'm man enough to admit that I've been confused about female genitalia. You never know what you're gonna get. You're always in dark light. And you always have to pretend to know what you're doing, so you never really get a good look. If I saw one coming at me in the light of day I'd probably take a snow shovel to it. Then she does the international cunnilingus sign and coaches me.

"It's like a flower. You have to unravel it."

So with the courage of Jacques Costeau on his last expedition, I started to unravel and unravel and unravel her huge coochie lips. It was like Dumbo. If she could flap them she would be able to fly out of the room and back to Germany. When I opened it all, it made a Tupperware burp.

And then my Thing, the little general, gets scared and starts talking to me again. "No. Hell no. I'm not going in there. I like the mouth."

But I didn't want to disappoint my pops, so I had to sacrifice the little general. In he went. I was like a porn star: "You like that street dick. That nasty Latin seed." So I started working her right in the fried chicken batter, this way and that way, up and down. And she's like, "No, over *here,* honey." "Oh, I'm sorry. It's my first time," I explained. Breast and thighs are flying up in the air—not hers, the chickens'. We're in a cloud of flour. And finally in her moment of orgasm, a stream flew out of her. I was soaking. Marinated in her juices.

"Hey, did you just . . . No, you didn't just . . . did you? I can't believe what I'm gonna say. Did you just pee on me?" I asked.

"No, it's the way I cum. It's another gift. See, my urethra is connected to my clitoris, and when my pubogeneous muscles contract . . . "

"You share too much, lady," I interrupted. "I just want to cuddle."

But my time was up, so she went over to the window, grabbed a coochie lip in each hand, and jumped. She flew away into the night like a giant pink bat. Bye, Mothra.

When I came out to the car, Pops was all questions. "How did you do? Give her the eighth ingredient, hijo?"

"Yeah, I did it!"

"But how do I know? I need proof," Pops persisted.

"Proof? Proof?" I wrang my shirt out and wiggled my toes, which made a squishy sound. "There's your proof."

"That's my boy!" Pops beamed. "Now we've shared this!"

F
r
e
a
k

DOMESTIC VIOLINS

I had become a man, and back home my moms was becoming her own woman—getting radical, going to college and using big words against my pops—acting like she was going places like some disco queen. Meanwhile, my pops wouldn't let his tenement dream die, so our house looked like a construction site, and he had to keep working at the **French restaurant.**

had become a man, and back home my moms was becoming her own woman—getting radical, going to college and using big words against my pops—acting like she was going places like some disco queen. Meanwhile, my pops wouldn't let his tenement dream die, so our house looked like a construction site, and he had to keep working at the French restaurant. It made my pops all stressed out, so he become the Grinch who stole Christmas. "There will be no laughter nor happiness again or singing in this house." And my moms got home one day and she's unnaturally happy.

She was humming, "Ah, freak out. Le chic. C'est freak."

Then the Grinch came back in. "Who said you could sing that thing? I am the king and *nothing* is what I say you should sing-sing sing! And you're late. That I really do hate. To be made to wait I don't appreciate. I just hate hate hate."

My moms looked tipsy and she took a big drag on her cigarette. "Ay, Fausto, you're being tan Dr. Seussian. Lateness is such an amorphous and bourgeois concept. But if you must know, Snoopy, it was 'cause I was swamped and backlogged with work and things," she said, taking off her high heels, "a ton of various sundry miscellaneousness-ness."

"And the day before you got here at midnight—what the hell was that about?" Pops demanded.

"See how hard I work for you?" said Moms, re-

L
e
g
u i z
a
m
o

moving her fake eyelashes. "I'm practically a slave. Lincoln, emancipate me. Break my shackles."

"Every time you're late I either think you're having an affair or you're dead. And when I call the Emergency Room in a panic and you're not dead, I get really pissed off. I need my woman home taking care of my childrens. Have you looked at them lately? John's sickly-looking and stupid, and Poochie's fat and ugly," said Pops.

"Look, Poochie would still be fat and ugly no matter what time I got home, so don't talk down to me. 'Cause I'm not just about reproduction anymore. I'm about me-production," Moms said as she brushed her hair. Mean.vhile, back in the kitchen, I'm like . . .

"Poochie, Dad called you fat and ugly and Mom agreed."

"Close that goddamn kitchen door!" Dad screamed. "Do you wanna be known as belt face for the rest of your life? Woman, don't make me have to teach you what respect is."

"Ay, fo, like a dishwasher could teach me anything," Moms spat back.

"Be quiet. Sssh! Do you wanna traumatize the childrens?"

Now Moms couldn't be stopped. "Okay, no more

talking! Quick, who am I?" and she mimed washing a dish.

My father dove at her and started choking her. She slapped him with one hand and choked him back with the other. And they start wrestling on the floor. It was just like watching the World Wrestling Federation on TV. "Sábado, sábado en Madison Square Garden. Lucha libre de la época. La gran pelea Leguizamo contra Leguizamo traído por Burger King el rey de las hamburguesas, y Baskin Robbins treinta y un sabores." It started to look like Moms was losing.

"I'm going to have to kill you," Pops yelled.

And Moms screamed, "You don't have to do anything you don't want. You're in America now."

I took my brother into the kitchen and said, "Yo, Poochie—Moms ain't doing so well. We got to double team him. You go in there and kick the shit out of him. And I'm a live on to tell the brave tale of how 'weak little fat boy' stood up to a ferocious maniac killer."

And Poochie stuttered, "B . . . b . . . b . . . But I can't."

"Poochie, this is no time to pretend to act like a retard," I said.

Then I see a shining big butcher steak knife that

my dad used on his father once before, so it's like a family heirloom. So I run out there like a little Jean Claude Goddamn.

I give Pops my best kung fu crouch and hold up the knife. "If you touch my moms or anyone in this house ever again, you're a goner."

"John, get outta here. You don't understand. This is none of your business," Pops yelled.

The butcher knife made me brave. "It is my business, so just get the fuck outta here! We're sick of you, Dad. Why don't you just get out and leave us all the fuck alone! Stop fucking up our lives and then taking it out on us. It's not our fault. Get out before we kill each other."

"You talk to your father like that," he seethed. "You're threatening me? You think you're man enough to take me, boy?"

"No, but I'm a do my best," I promised.

"Put that knife down," he demanded.

"No."

"Put it down."

Pops lunged at me and we struggled. I held onto that knife with both hands, but he got it away. "I hate you," I cried out, falling to my knees.

My father looked down at me. "I'm sorry, mi'jo, I

didn't mean to hurt you. I'm not a cruel person." He started putting on his hat and coat. "I hope your son never looks at you how you're looking at me. I'll leave. You know, John—I came here to work. I didn't come here to crawl, but I didn't care, 'cause all I ever wanted was milk for my kids and beer for me, and always remember in life there are no do-overs or repeats, so if you don't do what you want—you'll end up like me."

THIS was the Dad that I had been wanting all my life. And there he was standing there all exposed. And finally, for a brief second, I saw him for who he really was: a hurt child. And I knew he was gonna tell me the words I'd been waiting for my entire life, and he turns to me and says . . . "Your mom's a puta bitch!"

Moms staggered back in shock.

"I'm not a puta bitch, John," my moms protested.

"So, then where'd she get that fancy mink coat when you and Poochie look like boat people? Dressed in Saran Wrap. And why does she wear that cheap perfume and sequin tube tops and see-through hot pants?" he persisted.

"Ay, Fausto, please. I may be paradoxical and mercurial, but I'm a damn good time. And what do you do that's so epiphenal?"

"I'm the King of Tenements, as soon as I finish some of this construction around here . . . ," he trailed off.

"King of Tenements? You're the King of Holes, the Prince of Plaster. All I see around here is holes and plaster rock," Moms said contemptuously.

"That's it, Jezebel—get away from my childrens, you Salome, Samsonite and Delilah, get out of my house. You're a lousy wife, lousy cook, and all the big words in the world couldn't make you a good mother," Pops screamed. But he'd gone too far.

"Ex-cuseme. Ex-cuseme. Ex-cusme. 'Lousy mother' what? I gotta interfere on my own behalf, 'cause you can only fill a bottle so much before it spills over— and the lid just blew off this bottle!" My moms pushed me aside. "Move over, John. Fausto, ever since we've been together you've had the Midas touch in reverse—everything you touch turns to caca. I don't want your hand-me-down love, your second-hand affection, your leftover sex . . . You don't get me twice in a lifetime. I want to quench the fire in my soul. I'm not a mat to be stomped, a rag to be rung, oh God, I'm not happy nor sad. I . . . I . . . I can't breathe."

"Easy, woman—you're having a breakdown," my pops interrupted.

"No, Fausto, I'm having a breakthrough. Don't touch me. Don't confuse the end of your world with the beginning of mine. I have awakened. Not now, John—I'm freaking out. I only have one more thing to say to you. Where did I put that eight-track tape? Thank you, John. I dedicate this to all my sister girl-friends who have been compromised before me but gotten over in the end." And then she started singing the disco hit "I Will Survive." In the end, she flipped Pops the bird. "I'm gonna make up my own words, Fausto. I should've said this a long time ago. And listen good. You can't walk over me anymore. You want this fat ass, well, you can't have it anymore— aha. You made me into a bitch, Fausto, and I'm going to unbitch myself. No, Fausto, I can't be like other women. You know why, you wanna know why . . . ?" Just as the song was climaxing, Moms fell into a construction hole. "You and your holes, Fausto," she said, climbing out. Then she chimed in, again on the last few notes. "Hey, hey, Oh oh!" and she bowed and walked out.

That was a beautiful song and a nice moment for my moms, but unfortunately the house was under my father's name.

COLLEGE FIASCO

So my parents divorced and my father kicked us out of the house. And I went on my own to find my self. And I found out that I had a hard time being myself. I would rather be anybody than be myself. I would rather be anybody than be myself—so I went to college. I had gotten a perfect 1600 on my SATs, if you count all four times I took it, so I went to that hot bed of academia, the Learning Annex, to get an associate's degree in the Decline of West Coast Civilization.

So my parents divorced and my father kicked us out of the house. And I went on my own to find my self. And I found out that I had a hard time being myself. I would rather be anybody than be myself—so I went to college. I had gotten a perfect 1600 on my SATs, if you count all four times

I took it, so I went to that hot bed of academia, the Learning Annex, to get an associate's degree in the Decline of West Coast Civilization. And I was worried that I wasn't gonna fit in so I cleverly passed as a whiteboy, stayed out of the sun, straightened my hair, told people I was from California . . .

My surfer-boy act was not too convincing. "Malibu, to be exact. Oh, the rad waves, the whales, man, playing with dolphins, man, I communed with one. The things he shared with me. He explained the crimes of humanity in the name of tuna to me and I apologized."

So I got into a fraternity and at my initiation they kept trying to make me do shots and chug beer, but I was afraid if I did I would slip into urban, inner-city minority lingo. So I was like . . . "No thanks, dude, trying to cut back. Taper off. No, I got nothing to hide."

But then one of my fraternity brothers comes over with these mushrooms. I had no idea what they were. "Oh, cool, crudité. I love vegetables." All of a sudden, things slowed way down. "What the fuck is happening to me? Nighty night, rabbit." I collapsed on the floor laughing. Then I took a good look at my new frat brothers and I started laughing harder. "Yo, you are the whitest mothafuckers I ever saw. Please, tell me your shit is white. Coño. Puñeta. Shit something out of your pretty white ass!"

The room goes silent. They sense an ethnic in their midst. "I'm having a bad trip. Later, dudes, I got crazy munchies," I say, trying to pull it back together.

So I go pig out at the cafeteria, ready to feast, when out of my peripheral vision I saw a Latino brother from the West Coast. He had an aura you could hear.

"Órale vato, La Raza, Latina paz simone," he greeted me.

"Yo, waz up my Hispanic brother?" I said, shaking his hand.

"Shut up, stupid! Stop talking shit! It's Latino, you colonized eunuch. Hispanic is the slave name given to us by the Spaniards in Iberia, and Iberia is Phoenician for land of the rabbits. And do I look like a rabbit to you, motherfucker? Do you think you look like a furry rabbit, ese?" he hissed.

"I like carrots," I said.

He was my first militant orthodox feminist vegan radical Latino separatist.

"Shut up! Why are you eating the food of the op-pressor, ese?" he yelled.

"Chocolate pudding? Bill Cosby's black and he eats chocolate pudding," I defended myself.

F
r
e
a
k

....

"Shut up, stupid! Chocolate is oppressive, for it was pilfe . . . pilfereded . . . stolen from the temples of the Aztecs at the expense of thousands of warrior lives, homes. And it's an abomination, for it was forced to co-mingle with the Euro-fascist milk ripped from the bosom of innocent cows, which had been recently and peculiarly violated, simone," my Chicano brother ranted.

"Look, you gotta learn to talk regular to get by," I tried to point out, helpfully.

"I do talk regular," he said.

Just then my new trustafarian buds sauntered up. "Hey, *Jonathan,* is this suspicious character your bud?" one of them asked.

So I look them right in the eyes and muster up all my strength of will and character and say, "No. Oh, Jesus . . . I'm just directing him to his Affirmative Action booth. No poder hablar el español. No. No. Pero mucha graci-ass and de nalga," I say in my worst Spanish.

As we walked away, I saw a tear coming down the Chicano's face like that Indian in the sad garbage commercials. Anyway, I got kicked out of the fraternity cause my Chicano bro' outted me.

Leguizamo

JUILLIARD

After that, I figured my acting must need work and I started to take it a little more serious. So there I was, trying to get into Juilliard, one of the top acting schools, and I was there 'cause all the fine girls were there, too. So I do a Shakespeare monologue for my audition, which I fashioned from listening to **Sir John Gielgud records.**

After that, I figured my acting must need work and I started to take it a little more serious. So there I was, trying to get into Juilliard, one of the top acting schools, and I was there 'cause all the fine girls were there, too. So I do a Shakespeare monologue for my audition, which I fashioned from listening to Sir John Gielgud records. "Is this a dagger which I see before me the handle towards my hand come let me clutch thee."

But when I do it, it comes out like the ghetto classix. "Is this a dagger which I see before me? Yo, waz up with dat?"

Now I was on a roll. "What, ho! Ho. No, thou didn'tst. Thou besta talketh to thee back of thee hand, 'cause the fronteth ain't hearingth it, sirrah, out damned spot. My kingdom for a horse, or I wilst pimp slapeth thee and bitch slapeth thee. Oh, Juliet, alas alack, and a lick."

So I was rejected. The more rejection I got, the stronger I became—like some science fiction creature feeding on it.

I looked in the yellow pages and found Lee Strasberg was auditioning for his class, and there I am and all these actors are doing *Streetcar,* and all the women want to be Blanche DuBois and all the fellas want to be Brando. "Stella! Stella! What kind of queen do you think you are, sitting on that throne and swilling down my liquor. I say ha! Ha!"

After watching fifty Brandos, I knew I wouldn't pass, 'cause of my looks, so I didn't care. So I did my own take on it, Jerry Lewis style. And the acting teacher's like . . . "I survived the Holocaust, but I don't know if I can survive your performance. It's not very real. Dig deeper. Go to someplace painful in your past."

I immediately start wailing, "Poochie broke the antenna. It was Poochie."

I didn't get in there either, but I had found my gift: denial.

They may not have wanted me, but there was this Latina honey auditioning there—she remembered me and called me up. Her name was Boo Sanchez. She had a thick, home-girl accent. "I was nameded during Halloween, boo. Hilarious, right? Enough of me. My bad. And dog I was bugging when you went off, I mean . . . I loveded your Shakespeare—it was mad classical, right? Ai, please, I don't know what that jury's beef wichoo was, right? They are so mad corny? It was bomb. Pentameter. Iambic and all."

She got rejected, too. But we had each other. And I remembered what my grandfather said to me. He said to me, "John, you only get three loves in your life; don't waste them. Pull the plug." I used one up and the other one of mine had flown away. I wasn't gonna waste this one. Only thing is the mating ritual of the Latin woman is a little Jekyll and Hyde. We'd be sexing up and she'd be like, all of a sudden, "Animal, criminal, bestia, desgraciado, say you love me! Animal, criminal, zángano, sinberguenza, creído, arrogante, say you love me. Then lie. Lie the way you lied to get me here. I'm not in the mood anymore." Then she'd just stop and get water and pills.

"But baby, you said I was the best," I'd whine.

"No, no, I said you *did* your best. And besides, I have my gynecologist appointment tomorrow, and he told me not to have intercourse twenty-four hours ahead of time."

I saw a way around this. "Yeah, but you don't have a dentist appointment, do you?"

She was so self-sufficient and, honest, I fell madly, truly, and deeply in love. It was great to be with a real Latina who understood and completed me. Of course, my fear of intimacy drove my love away.

We'd be in the bathroom, getting ready for bed, and she'd start in. "Why you never say 'you love me'? I mean, I don't wanna make you say it . . ."

"Thank you, baby, 'cause I just feel . . . " And before I could even finish she'd say, "But I really think it would be in your best interest if you did. I just want it to come from you. I'm fine. It's not like I need it to get

L
e
g
u i z
a
m
o

by. It's not like I'm living in an emotional vacuum. A black hole. I'm cool. I'm straight. I'm . . . Why you so afraid to say it?"

"I'm not afraid of saying it. I just think I've proven myself through action. I mean, what could words possibly add? And I experience my emotions on a preverbal level. To refine them through language is to change and pollute them. Now you don't want me to say 'I love you' and stop our relationship dead in its tracks, do you?"

I thought I had her here.

"Yes. Kill it. I wanna hear those words. Even if I never see you again. I wanna hear those words!!!"

"You want me to say 'I love you'? There. Is that better?"

"What did your parents do to you? This is your father's fault. I'm calling him." She went for the phone, but I stopped her. "Then you call him and make him give you a sign that he loves you—or you're never gonna be a man. All your life you're gonna feel guilty and alone unless he releases you. It's awful not to be loved. It's the worst thing in the world. I oughta know. You never say you love me to me. I hate you. Why are you so withholding? You really hurt me, John." She started sobbing. "I hate you. I hate my life. I wish I

. . . .

were dead." Then she'd scream at such a high pitch it was silent. When Latin women get upset, only dogs can hear them. So I'd ask my dog. "What she say, boy?"

Astro would let me know. "That bitch has had enough of your shit."

Thanx, boy. So I leave her alone hoping she'll calm down and go into the living room for some food and I'm watching TV and she walks in and yells, "Who the hell told you you could watch my television!? And get off that couch. You know it's only for the guests!!"

I don't know how she got by the bubble wrap, but she did. And then the warm urine of realization flowed down my leg—holy shit, she's just like my pops. Well, I already had a father; I certainly didn't need that nonsense in a girlfriend. So I ended that mierda right there.

"Will you marry me?" I asked.

I know. I know. See, they tell you your whole life that you always marry your moms. Well, not me—I was gonna marry my pops.

L
e
g
u i z
a
m
o

AGENT

So now my personal life was spoken for and I was looking for direction in my life, and I read in the paper that there was an open call and I met with this casting agent. I put on my lucky interview suit and **went for it.**

So now my personal life was spoken for and I was looking for direction in my life, and I read in the paper that there was an open call and I met with this casting agent. I put on my lucky interview suit and went for it. "So what's the word?" I asked him.

"You're too ethnic. That's the word. What am I supposed to do with you? Start a reservation? They don't want a Hispanic—they want someone who can *play* a Hispanic. Wait—how do you feel about playing junkies?"

And I said, "Search no more, feast your eyes . . . Stop the world, I'm down."

L
e
g
u i z
a
m
o

So, bam, I'm in my first play. I show up at the theater for the first rehearsal all cocky, and the director's going...'More Latino. I wanna feel the agony and patheticness of your people." I'm really trying, you know. "I need a fix, man—come on, take my kid, anything." "More pathetic, more Latino. More junkie, **think Latino!" the director yells.**

So, *bam,* I'm in my first play. I show up at the theater for the first rehearsal all cocky, and the director's going . . . "More Latino. I wanna feel the agony and patheticness of your people."

So I'm really trying, giving it all

I got. "I need a fix, man—come on, take my kid, any-thing."

"More pathetic, more Latino. More junkie, think Latino!" the director yells.

"I'm outta veins, I'll stick it in my neck, how about my eyeball? La metadona está cabrona." I'm eager to please.

"That's it. You're the Latin guy I was looking for. You got the job," he said.

PYRO-
TECHNIX
CLIMACTIC
FINALE

So it's opening night for *A Junkie for All Seasons*, I'm in my dressing room; a shower curtain's hanging up backstage with a mirror and flashlight, it's sleazy, grimy, and nasty, and I'm getting into character, "The vein, I missed it. I'm jonesing." There's a knock at my shower curtain and Pops walks in. "Hey, open up in there. You're not doing what I think you're doing in there."

So it's opening night for *A Junkie for All Seasons.* I'm in my dressing room; a shower curtain's hanging up backstage with a mirror and flashlight. It's sleazy, grimy, and nasty, and I'm getting into character, "The vein, I missed it. I'm jonesing."

There's a knock at my shower

curtain and Pops walks in. "Hey, open up in there. You're not doing what I think you're doing in there."

"Dad? Hey, Dad, waz up?" I hugged him. "It's great to see ya. You never returned my calls, never wrote, nothing. It's all right. I never took it personally. What brings you here?"

"My new kids wanted to see the show," he said.

"Oh," I said, disappointed.

"My Junior is so much better looking and funny, more talented, more intelligent than you ever were. That's why he's the best in his acting class." Pops beamed proudly.

And I get that look on my face like when you wanna fart without making noise. Pops went on. "I always said if anybody can make something out of nothing, it's you, John. Let's be honest. I know you never liked me."

"I like you, Dad."

"Come on, John, you don't like me," he insisted.

"Dad, you're my father—I gotta like you."

"No, you don't like me. Come on, be a man. Tell me."

"You know, I always thought if I had the father the other kids had, the perfect father, then I wouldn't be so alone. Like when Randy Garcia's father came home their house would fill with laughter. Dad, I'm always waiting for you, waiting for something to be different, waiting for you to be my hero, waiting for you to do one little thing that's gonna help me forgive you. But you always fuck it up."

Or actually I thought I said that; then I realized nothing had come out.

So, he was like, "John. You know I'm not too crazy about you, either. We were never meant to be father and son, but then who the hell really is? We're probably never gonna get along. But that doesn't mean I don't love the shit out of you, even if I can't stand the sight of you. Now go out there and be the best junkie you can be and give me a kiss."

And I thought, "Is that all I am? Is that all I am to you?" And I flashed back to when I saw *Chorus Line.* Morales wouldn't have been a party to this goddamn spic-ploitation, hustler, junkie, pimp, down-and-outer sucker profanity! The stage manager yelled, "You're on in five." And all of a sudden I allowed myself to want more for myself, to be more and do more, master of my own destiny, never wait for anyone, take life into my own hands, like my father had once wanted for me and like all the Moraleses, Morenos, Arnazs, Puentes, Cheechs and Chongs before me;

F
r
e
a
k
. . . .

124

who had to eat it, live it, get fed up with it, finesse it, scheme it, even Machiavelli it, to get out from under all the ills that Latin flesh is heir to and who dug right down to the bottom of their souls to turn nothing into something. I dedicate this to all of you.

And I think back to sitting with Pops on the fire escape and he says to me again, "Come on, give me a kiss. What are y'fraid of, a little affection?"

"All right, Dad." And I kiss him.

"Not on the lips, you little freak."

And I dedicate this to you, too, Dad.

L
e
g
u i z
a
m
o

. . . .

125

ABOUT THE
AUTHORS

John Leguizamo is an actor and comedian, best known for his award-winning one-man shows *Mambo Mouth* and *Spic-O-Rama*, which ran off-Broadway to great critical and commercial success. He starred in the comic television show *House of Buggin'* and in *Spawn, Romeo and Juliet, To Wong Foo, Carlito's Way, The Pest*, and many other movies.

David Bar Katz is a writer/director and cofounder of Lower East Side Films. A graduate of Williams College, he lives in Alphabet City, a few blocks from John Leguizamo and from a vacant lot that used to be his great-grandfather's Yiddish theater.